SERIES EDITOR: LEE JOHNSON

OSPREY MILITARY MEN-AT-ARM

US MARINE CORPS IN WORLD WAR I 1917–1918

FIRST IN
THE FIGHT–   ALWAYS
FAITHFUL–
BE A U.S.MARINE!
ENLIST AT
24 EAST 23RD STREET, NEW YORK CITY

TEXT BY
MARK R. HENRY

COLOUR PLATES BY
DARKO PAVLOVIĆ

First published in Great Britain in 1999 by Osprey Publishing, Elms Court, Chapel Way, Botley, Oxford OX2 9LP

ISBN 1 85532 852 6

Editor: Martin Windrow
Design: Black Spot
Origination: Valhaven Ltd, Isleworth, UK
Printed through World Print Ltd., Hong Kong

99 00 01 02 03   10 9 8 7 6 5 4 3 2 1

For a catalogue of all books published by Osprey Military, Automotive and Aviation please write to:

The Marketing Manager, Osprey Publishing, P.O. Box 140, Wellingborough, Northants, NN8 4ZA, United Kingdom

OR VISIT OSPREY'S WEBSITE AT: www.osprey-publishing.co.uk

Dedication

I would like to dedicate this book to Pvt Richard Henry and Sgt Edwin T. Beach, both veterans of the 23rd Co/6th Machinegun Battalion. *Semper Fidelis*.

Author's note & acknowledgements

In this text I use the USMC Museum designation of 'Pattern' for uniforms and equipment made especially for the Corps, e.g. P1917. US Army issue items are designated by 'Model' date, e.g. M1917.

The author would like to recognize and thank the following individuals and organisations for their assistance: Ed Rogers, Grant Sigsworth, Robert Hargis, Ellen Guillemette, Charles Archuletta, Bob Queen, Jerry Beach, Emil Stefanacci, Doug Bailey, R.Smallwood-Roberts, Carol and James Henry, Garry James, Mike Rudder, Judy Petsch, Larry Corbett, Lena Kaljot, B.Omanson, Karl George, Bruce Norton, CPO Hacala; Great War Militaria, Sam Houston State University, Mr King and Bara-King Photos, USN Bureau of Medicine, USMC Museum and Historical Center. I would especially like to thank the USMC Recruit Depot Museum (San Diego) and Ken Smith-Christmas of the Marine Corps Museum Branch (Quantico). Unless otherwise stated, all photos are from US National Archives or USMC sources.

Publishers' note

Readers may wish to study this title in conjunction with the following Osprey publications:

MAA 80 *The German Army 1914–18*
MAA 81 *The British Army 1914–18*
MAA 182 *British Battle Insignia 1914–18*
MAA 205 *US Army Combat Equipments 1910–88*
MAA 245 *British Territorial Units 1914–18*
MAA 286 *The French Army 1914–18*
Elite 24 *The Old Contemptibles*
Warrior 12 *The German Stormtrooper 1914–18*
Warrior 16 *The British Tommy 1914–18*
Campaign 11 *Kaiserschlacht 1918*
Campaign 49 *Mons 1914*
Campaign 58 *First Ypres 1914*

Artist's note

Readers may care to note that the original paintings from which the colour plates in this book were prepared are available for private sale. All reproduction copyright whatsoever is retained by the Publishers. All enquiries should be addressed to:

Darko Pavlović, Modecova 3, 10090 Zagreb, Croatia

The Publishers regret that they can enter into no correspondence upon this matter.

TITLE PAGE **A Marine officer as he appeared for 'colonial' service, c.1917; by 1918 he would look very different in the trenches of the Western Front. This recruiting poster clearly shows the officer's pattern russet leather gear which will soon be exchanged for webbing equipment.**

US MARINE CORPS IN WORLD WAR I 1917–1918

INTRODUCTION

A United States Army major was visiting the wounded in a French hospital in the environs of Paris in 1918. When the doctors proudly escorted him to the bedside of a wounded doughboy, he asked the young soldier if he was indeed an American. 'No sir,' he replied, 'I'm a Marine'.

This exchange is exemplary of the pride that a US Marine takes in his identity as a member of the Corps. In 1918 the Marines had to struggle to maintain that distinctive identity within the huge American Expeditionary Force in France; but they were to earn a fighting reputation second to none in their battles at Belleau Wood, Soissons, St Mihiel, Blanc Mont and the Meuse-Argonne. The eminent US Army historian S.L.A.Marshall was to describe these Marines as '... a little raft of sea soldiers in an ocean of Army that was without doubt the most aggressive body of diehards on the Western Front'. After their initial encounters in combat the Germans gave the Marines the nickname of 'Devil Dogs'. This book is not, however, directly concerned with the battle history of the 4th Marine Brigade or its parent 2nd Division of the AEF. What follows is a guide to the organisation, uniforms and equipment of the US Marine Corps in Europe in 1917–18.

ORGANISATION

Following the US declaration of war in April 1917, the recruiting offices of the Marine Corps were mobbed by enthusiastic volunteers eager to become – as the Marine recruiting posters trumpeted – 'First to Fight'. The Marine Corps, a branch of the Navy, demanded high standards of intelligence and physical fitness. All recruits had to be able to read, write and understand English (not a requirement too obvious to mention in a period when millions of foreign immigrants had only arrived in the USA fairly recently). They had to be at least 18 years old, of sound mind and body, with good eyesight and hearing and 'at least twenty teeth'. The minimum acceptable height was 5ft 4ins, and the minimum weight 124lbs. Only one in ten volunteers were accepted. They could enlist for a four-year 'hitch' or the duration of hostilities.

One new recruit described his basic training: 'The first day I was afraid that I was going to die. The next two weeks my sole fear was that I was not going to die. And after that, I knew I'd never die, because I'd become so hard that nothing could kill me.' Marksmanship was highly prized in the Marines, and about half of the recruit's eight-week training

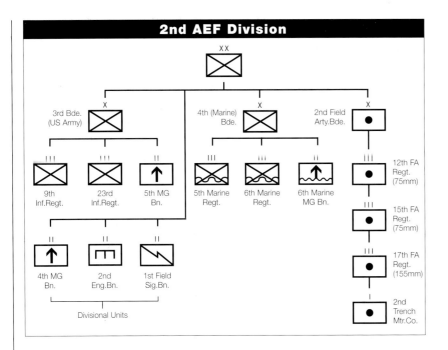

2nd AEF Division

XX

- **3rd Bde. (US Army)** (X)
  - 9th Inf.Regt.
  - 23rd Inf.Regt.
  - 5th MG Bn.
  - 4th MG Bn.
  - 2nd Eng.Bn.
  - 1st Field Sig.Bn.
  - *Divisional Units*
- **4th (Marine) Bde.** (X)
  - 5th Marine Regt.
  - 6th Marine Regt.
  - 6th Marine MG Bn.
- **2nd Field Arty.Bde.** (X)
  - 12th FA Regt. (75mm)
  - 15th FA Regt. (75mm)
  - 17th FA Regt. (155mm)
  - 2nd Trench Mtr.Co.

was conducted on the rifle range. Most Marines received their basic training at Parris Island, South Carolina, and some advanced training at the new base at Quantico, Virginia. The infant Marine Militia/Reserve, with a strength of under 1,000 men, could make only a limited impression on the Corps' new manpower needs. A few American Indians were enrolled in the Corps, but no blacks. Women Marines were enlisted as auxiliaries in small numbers, but they never left the States. Late in the war, the Corps accepted draftees who volunteered for the Marines. They retained the right to refuse men who failed to measure up to their recruiting standards.

The 5th and 6th Marine Regiments were specially organised for service in France, as was the 6th Machinegun Battalion. The 5th

A 'devil dog Marine' of the 67th Company, 1st Battalion, 5th Regiment. Another company of the 5th Marines acquired an anteater as a mascot. When he refused to eat ants, further research revealed him to be a coatimundi – a friendly South American mammal resembling a stretched racoon, whose preferred diet is fruit, eggs and lizards.

4

US Army Gen.Bundy with Col.Catlin of the 6th Marine Regiment. Catlin was a survivor of the USS *Maine* disaster of 1898, and held the Medal of Honor for service at Vera Cruz, Mexico, in 1914. Both wear British SBR gasmasks and steel helmets; note Col.Catlin's shirt collar exposed to ease the chafing of the tunic collar, and the pointed pocket flaps of his forest green tunic.

Regiment was formed rapidly, with a fairly high percentage of veteran Marines recalled from duty around the world. It began arriving in France in June 1917. In the 6th Regiment: 'The officers, from captain up, and 50 or so NCOs were old-time Marines, but the junior officers and all of the privates were new men ... 60% of the entire regiment were college men.' The last elements of the 6th arrived in France by February 1918. The 11th and 13th Regiments (5th Brigade) were also raised for war service, but they were assigned logistical duties in France and saw no action. The Marines also formed an artillery regiment – the 10th – for service in France, but this unit was still in the USA when the war ended.

The senior officer ranks were filled with experienced Marines of long expeditionary (colonial) experience; in fact, both the 5th and 6th Regiments were commanded by Medal of Honor winners. The junior officer ranks were hastily filled out with recent college graduates, a number of whom were famous athletes and sportsmen. Additionally, a

Composition of US Marine Forces in France, 1917–18

4TH (MARINE) BRIGADE, AEF

Fifth Regiment

1st Bn	2nd Bn	3rd Bn
17th Co	8th Co	16th Co
49th Co	43rd Co	20th Co
66th Co	51st Co	45th Co
67th Co	55th Co	47th Co
	8th Machinegun Co	

Sixth Regiment

1st Bn	2nd Bn	3rd Bn
74th Co	78th Co	82nd Co
75th Co	79th Co	83rd Co
76th Co	80th Co	84th Co
95th Co	96th Co	97th Co
	73rd Machinegun Co	

Sixth Machinegun Battalion

15th Co	77th Co
23rd Co	81st Co

5th (Marine) Brigade, AEF
Eleventh Regiment
Thirteenth Regiment
Fifth Machinegun Battalion

1st Marine Aviation Force
4 squadrons

small number of Marine NCOs were commissioned; and volunteer Army officers were detailed to the Marine Brigade upon its arrival in France. After the battle of Belleau Wood more enlisted Marines were commissioned; and Marine officers also began to serve in small numbers in Army units of the 2nd Division, and in other units throughout the AEF.

General John J. Pershing, commander of the AEF, had stipulated that all US units in Europe be created big. The infantry company consisted of six officers and 250 men. It was led by a captain, and had four 58-strong rifle platoons and an 18-man HQ detachment; the platoon had four 12-man sections and a HQ section. The Marines entered the war with companies designated by numbers; these numbered companies were redesignated in US Army fashion by letter and battalion – for example, the 49th Company, 5th Regiment became B Company, 1st Battalion, 5th Regiment. Marines disliked this redesignation, and did not fully embrace it until after the war.

Each battalion was commanded by a major and had an establishment of 26 officers and 1,027 men in four companies. Pershing was careful to keep AEF units up to strength with replacements after each battle. In July 1918 he ordered – in line with the similar practice in other Allied armies – that 10% of each battalion be kept out of the line during major attacks; this '10 per' rule gave units more of a cadre to reform around if they were particularly hard hit. An AEF regiment was commanded by a colonel and had three battalions, a 178-man machine gun company (with 12-plus guns), a supply company and a HQ company. The regimental headquarters company had eight officers and 336 men in five platoons: HQ/band, signal, 3in mortar, engineer, and a platoon of three 37mm guns.

The AEF (Marine) Brigade followed standard organisation, with two infantry regiments and a machine gun battalion. It was commanded by a brigadier-general (one star), and its strength of 8,400 put it on a par with the combat strength of a British or French division by this stage of the war. The French high command took to treating a US division (28,000 men) as effectively an army corps.

It is important to point out that the 4th Marine Brigade in the 2nd AEF Division had the regular US Army 3rd Brigade (9th and 23rd Infantry Regiments) as its partner in all its fights. These two brigades respected each other's fighting prowess, and were in such fierce competition with one another as to be called the 'Racehorse Brigades'. The artillery, engineer and other combat support elements within the division were provided by the Army. The US Navy provided the medical support for the Marines (as they still do).

With the imminent arrival in France of the 5th Marine Brigade (11th and 13th Regiments), Marine Maj. Gen. John A. Lejeune, the 2nd Division commander, asked for permission to form an all-Marine division. Pershing wisely refused, and these new arrivals sat out the last days of the war on supply and support duties. As Lejeune was later to realize, the Corps did not yet have the manpower to fully outfit and maintain a division in the line in a major European war.

A Marine company was assigned as a Paris Military Police unit. Another company was employed as Gen. Pershing's 'palace guard' at his HQ at Chaumont, additional Marines being assigned as escorts, drivers and orderlies. Pershing's Marines, and many others who had been

Gunner Henry L.Hulbert was born in Kingston-upon-Hull, England, in 1867. He joined the US Marines in 1898 and won the Medal of Honor in Samoa a year later. Here he wears the classic Marine officer's forest green uniform with the collar 'bombs' marking warrant officer's rank.

OPPOSITE **Typical appearance of an AEF Marine after the Belleau Wood battle of June 1918. He wears Army drab uniform, a British helmet and gasmask satchel, but no insignia identifying him as a member of the Corps.**

detailed away from the 2nd Division on various duties, were returned in September 1918; the Paris Marines returned to the division just before the Meuse-Argonne offensive late that October.

The Marine Corps also provided four squadrons of aircraft. The fledgling 1st Marine Aviation Force was formed in northern France with 36 DH-4 and DH-9A light bombers. While the Marine crews waited for their aircraft to arrive they flew with the RAF's Nos.217 and 218 Squadrons. By the Armistice they had dropped 33,000lbs of bombs, shot down four German aircraft and claimed a further eight.

True to their sea-going origins, Marines served on US Navy ships which formed a part of the Allied North Sea Fleet. The Marine contingent on a battleship consisted of one or two officers and 50 men. Besides various other duties, they crewed several of the ship's 5in secondary guns. Shipboard Marines were deployed into Russia at Archangel, Murmansk and Vladivostok in 1918 during the Allied intervention in the Russian Civil War. These men joined other Allied troops in the questionable task of guarding war materials and keeping the peace; the last of them left Vladivostok in 1922.

UNIFORMS

Pattern P1912/17 Marine Uniform

This forest green wool uniform was unique to the Marine Corps. Its design resembled the US Army Model 1912 uniform: the tunic had a plain standing collar, epaulettes and four patch pockets, the breast pockets pleated and the skirt pockets of the 'bellows' type. Dark bronze buttons bearing star, eagle and anchor devices, essentially unchanged since 1804, were used throughout. The pointed cuffs of this uniform have become a standard feature of Marine coats. The almost identical P1912 Marine tunic might also be seen in France, usually with the originally absent skirt pockets added. In late 1918 a hole was punched in each side of the collar of the P1917 tunic to take the new collar badges. A dark brown leather belt with an open brass buckle was sometimes worn with this tunic.

Marines were issued matching forest green long trousers with side seam pockets and belt loops; these were worn with a steamed crease. The waistband size was adjustable at the rear by a two-piece cloth strap and brass buckle. A one-inch-wide khaki web belt with a dark bronze open frame buckle was worn with the trousers. The enlisted men initially wore tall (seven-stud) P1911 lace-up khaki canvas leggings in France. These had a leather instep strap; and were sometimes scrubbed with salt water to give them an 'old salt' look. The men and many of the officers changed over to British issue drab puttees before going into the trenches.

Officers wore the same wool tunic as the men, with the addition of rank insignia and subdued bronze eagle, globe and anchor collar badges (NB – hereafter in this text the USMC eagle, globe and anchor device is abbreviated to EGA.) The tunic was sometimes made in lighter wearing barathea material for use in the field. Regulation legwear were matching breeches, sometimes made of whipcord material, worn with leather 'clamshell' Stohwasser gaiters; the inseam reinforcement was of

Col.Harry White (Staff) wears the officer's 'special' full dress with fringed bullion epaulettes, c.1915. His rank is shown by the cuff and epaulette detail. The sword knot – like the cords worn by officers on the campaign hat – is mixed gold and red.

doubled cloth, not leather. Officers' tailored uniforms were privately purchased both in the USA and in Paris.

Though initially not considered a regulation item, the British-style **Sam Browne** belt was immediately purchased upon arrival in France by AEF officers. It was universally recognized by all combatants in Europe as the symbol of officer rank; indeed, a 'Sam Browne' was the AEF nickname for an officer. To this day it is worn by Marine officers on special occasions. Despite Gen.Pershing's embrace of the belt in Europe, the Army refused to recognize the Sam Browne as regulation wear stateside, and MPs even waited on the docks to divest returning officers of the offending item. Marine officers, to the chagrin of their Army fellows, were authorized to retain their belts.

P1912 Marine Khaki Uniform

This 'tropical' uniform was made of a medium khaki-coloured light cotton/canvas material. It was cut to the same pattern as the P1912 wool uniform, and was worn with P1911 leggings. During the summer of 1917 the 5th Marines wore this uniform during embarkation. Tunics issued after 1914 had skirt pockets added (P1915?). It was common to wear the khaki cotton trousers and the P1904/17 woollen shirt without the tunic for fatigue and daily wear in the tropics.

RIGHT **Quartermaster Sergeant Detrich, 5th Marines; note the rank insignia of three chevrons over three stripes on the sleeve of his issue P1912 overcoat. He is armed with a Colt M1911 semi-automatic pistol, as were most senior NCOs of the Corps.**

Model 1912/1917 Army (AEF) Uniform

This drab wool four-pocket uniform was declared the AEF standard by Gen.Pershing in January 1918, 'drab' in this context meaning a colour varying between a dusty brown and a mustard brown/green. This Army uniform was supplied to the Marines in France in early 1918; however, they continued to wear their P1917 uniforms. The Army M1912 tunic had straight cuffs, epaulettes, and dark bronze buttons bearing the National Eagle. The standing collar fronts had holes punched for the two Army dark bronze insignia disks. Enlisted Marines, having no collar insignia, wore their collars plain. The M1917 version of this tunic was of a slightly simplified pattern, and the M1918 even more so: the four pocket flaps were retained, but the pockets were now internal to the tunic. British tunics were also issued to the AEF in limited numbers to make up for uniform shortages. The rough woollen material used in the M1917 uniforms produced during the war was of almost blanket quality.

Drab wool breeches were worn with this tunic by all ranks, closed tight to the lower leg by laces. Late in the war straight-legged trousers became available. Marines universally wore drab puttees with this uniform.

Dress Uniforms

Though strictly beyond the scope of this book, a short description of dress uniforms is in order. The Marine dress uniform of World War I was not dissimilar to that worn to the present day, and was influenced by British styles. The enlisted man's tunic was of dark blue wool and cut basically similar to the forest green P1912 tunic except for the absence of pockets. It was piped in red, and had added three-button cuff flaps; NCOs wore oversized yellow silk rank and service stripes, and all ranks received collar EGAs after the war. It was worn with a whitened buff leather belt with a plain brass rectangular buckle. The uniform was completed by sky blue trousers, with one-inch red side stripes for NCOs, and the blue, red-piped P1897 visored bell-crowned cap – see Plate A1. Full dress was not issued to Marines headed for France.

Officers wore a slightly longer undress blue coat without red piping. Sky blue trousers were worn by all Marines except for staff officers and generals, who wore dark blue; officers had a 1.5in wool leg stripe. The traditional Mameluke-style sword on a gold-laced sword belt was carried by officers on formal occasions; NCOs wore the P1859 sergeant's sword. Officers' full dress included a double-breasted dark blue coat with gold-laced standing collar, gold embroidered cuff galloons and gold shoulder knots. They also had a short mess dress and a summer white uniform.

Cold Weather Uniforms

A long forest green double-breasted wool overcoat (P1912) was initially worn by Marines in France. An unofficial shortened pea jacket version of this was also used as a 'deck coat' aboard ship. By 1918, Marines were using the Army M1918 overcoat. This was a drab double-breasted wool overcoat which had been shortened to about the knee to make it lighter

Col.'Whispering Buck' Neville (Medal of Honor, Vera Cruz) commanded the 5th Marines in France. Neville became the 14th Commandant of the Corps in 1928. Of note are his 'aviator' or field boots; and his hat EGA, which is crooked here, with the anchor vertical.

and to keep the skirts out of the mud. The older coats had a buttoned cuff tab. NCO stripes were sometimes worn on overcoats.

A short reefer style double-breasted 'Mackinaw' was also worn, especially by drivers, but was rarely available to line troops. This shawl-collared drab wool coat was hip-length and sported large plain bone buttons and two skirt patch pockets. Mackinaws were popular among some AEF officers; Army General Douglas MacArthur was noted for wearing one.

Drab knit sweaters were issued to be worn under the tunic in cold weather; these pullovers were available in both long-sleeved and sleeveless versions. Knit wool scarfs, toques and fingerless gloves were also used; many of these knit items were provided by the Red Cross/YWCA and came in drab or grey. British leather jerkins or US copies were sometimes used when available. Drab wool vests were also purchased and used, though these were rare.

Officers initially wore the long double-breasted P1912 overcoat, with a complex pattern of black cord cuff trim based on rank, and large Marine buttons. Rank insignia were worn on the epaulettes. In a famous AEF story, the Marine brigade commander General 'Whispering Buck' Neville had his forest green overcoat destroyed by an over-eager souvenir hunter. The general had hung his coat out to dry while he went inside a recently captured bunker to talk to an Army colonel. A passing Army muleskinner spotted the fancy 'German' general's overcoat hanging near the door of this bunker, and hacked off the arms; he was proudly mounting them on the ears of his mule just as Neville emerged from the bunker looking for his overcoat. Needless to say, the general was less than amused. This type of coat was soon retired in favour of trenchcoats, Burberrys, mackinaws and M1918 short coats.

A rain poncho was worn by Marines in their first European winter of 1917/18. It was soon replaced by a treated drab canvas long raincoat (M1907) in early 1918 – this popular unlined 'slicker' was found to be easier to wear in combat than the poncho, and was also worn in the summer as a 'duster coat'. This coat had metal claw closures instead of buttons, and a large right hip patch pocket.

ABOVE, LEFT **Marines training with the French M2 gasmask. Note the semi-circular linen gasmask bag; and, bottom centre, the folded rim of the Marine campaign hat.**

ABOVE **This striking-looking officer is Gen.C.Doyen, a 34-year veteran of the Corps and the first commander of the 4th Marine Brigade in 1917; he wears the earlier P1912 forest green tunic which had no skirt pockets, and sports a French M1915 Adrian helmet, which was a stylish choice for senior US officers in the first year of the war. In this instance the helmet bears the chasseurs' buglehorn device, but it was probably acquired at random. He also wears Stohwasser gaiters, and carries a French M2 gasmask.**

1917: A Marine sergeant washes his 'dogs' in front of his two-man 'pup' tent. A seabag and mess equipment can be seen at left; and note the hobnail boots of the sleeping Marine.

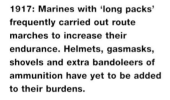

1917: Marines with 'long packs' frequently carried out route marches to increase their endurance. Helmets, gasmasks, shovels and extra bandoleers of ammunition have yet to be added to their burdens.

Headgear

Both the Army and the Marines wore the Montana peaked or 'lemon squeezer' campaign hat upon their arrival in France. The brown P1912 Marine version of this hot weather hat had a folded rim which was evident on the underside. A large EGA was worn on the centre front, to which Reserve officers added a bronze 'R'. Red and gold mixed hat cords were worn by officers; enlisted ranks wore no cords. This hat was sometimes worn with a narrow leather chinstrap.

Initial training in France was conducted in French Adrian helmets, but British Mk I (Brodie) steel helmets were provided to the Marines in early 1918, and the slightly modified M1917 American version was soon

A veteran French captain – the three sleeve 'sardines' indicate more than two years at the front – explains the VB grenade discharger cup to Marines; the discharger's carrying case lies in the middle of the table. Marine P1917 uniforms with campaign hats and leggings suggest a date of 1917.

to be available. The M1917 manganese steel helmet was issued in a sand-roughened drab green finish; Marines commonly repainted their helmets a darker forest green. In the trenches, helmets painted with irregular block camouflage patterns (copied from the widespread German practice) were not unknown, but rare. The hat EGA was sometimes mounted on the front of helmets, but this was uncommon, although it became regulation after the war. The leather chinstrap was sometimes worn behind the head or over the front brim.

This sniper has an '03' with a Winchester A5 telescopic sight. His sergeant's chevrons would be dark drab on light drab when in shirtsleeve order.

French chasseurs à pied watch a member of the 5th Marines show off his prowess with the .45 pistol (which was fired one-handed until the 1970s). The French were usually amazed at Marine marksmanship, but considered it a superfluous skill in modern war. This Marine wears both a rifle cartridge belt and a pistol holster.

The 'overseas hat' or sidecap was introduced into the AEF in early 1918, inspired by French and to a lesser extent British practice, to replace the campaign hat. This drab wool cap was provided or procured in any number of variants on the basic pattern. The British style had two small buttons on the front of the curtain or turban. Marines wore their hat EGA on the left front; small bronze regimental numbers were sometimes worn just below the EGA or on the opposite side (as were, reportedly, even company numbers in some cases). Pulled down so that the crown section expanded, this cap could be worn under the helmet for extra warmth. An enlisted forest green version was produced after the war. Shipboard Marines and officers retained their visored P1897 bell crown hats in forest green.

Officers wore this same cap made in drab or forest green, commonly piped in red; generals' caps were trimmed in gold. EGA and officer rank were worn in any number of ways, but rank on the left side and EGA on the right was the most common.

A Marine's hair was worn short, with moustaches both short and uncommon. Men wearing glasses were rarely enlisted, but round frame glasses were to be seen among older Marines.

Shirts and Shoes

The two-pocket Marine P1904/1917 shirt was made of a light woollen flannel in a khaki drab colour. At first glance it appears to be a pullover due to the design of the placket, but it had a full-length front opening. Its pocket flaps were pointed, unlike those of the Army shirt. Marines

also wore the slightly darker Army M1916 pullover woollen shirt. Both shirts had elbow patches, and five bone/plastic front buttons. NCO sleeve insignia were worn in drab on light drab backing. Due to the scratchiness of the tunic collars the wearing of the shirt collar exposed over the tunic collar was very common. When shirts were worn by officers without tunics they sported a drab necktie and small paired rank insignia on the collar.

US M1904/06/10 russet brown ankle boots were initially used by the AEF in France. These were found to be too lightly constructed to stand up to the rugged conditions of the Western Front. Gen.Pershing initially obtained French and English boots as a stop-gap measure until the US M1917/1918 (Pershing) boots could be provided. These new 4.5in-high ankle boots were based on a combined US and French pattern, and the brown leather showed the 'rough side out'. They had reinforced hobnailed soles and metal 'horseshoes' on the heels, and seven lace eyelets on a side. They were heavily treated or greased for weatherproofing. British boots (described as heavy and stiff) were again issued to the Marine Brigade just after the Armistice in time for the forced road marches to the Rhine in late 1918. High-top rubber boots and hip waders might also be used in the trenches.

Officers might wear any number of boots for field use, from the issue M1918 to special aviator style lace-up field boots of knee length. The regulation Stohwasser leather gaiters were also worn in the trenches. Full length dark brown riding boots with nickel spurs were worn by mounted officers on parade.

Hospital Corpsmen and Chaplains

All the medical personnel in a Marine unit were provided by the US Navy; these naval hospital corpsmen served in the front lines with the Marine rifle companies as well as in unit aid stations. They used the same mix of P1917 and AEF M1912 uniforms as the Marines; collar

insignia were not worn, their branch being identified by a red cross brassard on the left arm. The NCOs wore their Navy rank patches on the left sleeve, with the white eagle ('crow') facing to the rear. Pharmacist's mates (NCOs) and hospital corpsmen were the two medical ratings. Both a dark blue patch incorporating the eagle, a red cross and red rating stripes, and a black-on-tan version, were commonly worn; a forest green version also existed. Marine or Army NCO stripes were also seen. Stretcher bearers were initially Navy medical personnel or Marine bandsmen, but after Belleau Wood they were replaced by detailed Marines; bearers wore either a blue brassard with white 'LB' for Litter Bearer, or more commonly the red-cross-on-white armband.

Naval medical doctors acted as unit surgeons and dentists. They wore the Marine officer's uniform and insignia while serving with the Marines. Along with collar EGAs, Navy doctors sometimes wore the medical corps caduceus. Naval officers attached to the Marines were referred to by their equivalent Marine ranks. Chaplains also wore Marine officer's uniform with the addition of a cross on the collar.

A Marine company would have between two and five hospital corpsmen with a pharmacist's mate as the company corpsman; a battalion aid station would have five to seven men and a chief. Doctors might work at battalion or regimental aid stations. Marine Brigade hospital corpsmen received two Medals of Honor, 55 Navy Crosses, 33 Distinguished Service Crosses, 237 Silver Stars and numerous foreign decorations, and were among the most decorated US organisations of the war.

(In addition to frontline medics, the French used specially trained dogs to provide first aid – and cigarettes! These animals would stop by the wounded, who could remove bandages and water from the small packs they carried. Marines encountered these first aid dogs at Belleau Wood.)

BELOW **Verdun front, spring 1918: two Corpsmen treat a wounded Marine in the trenches. Although the Marines were broken in by being deployed to a quiet sector in March 1918, a steady trickle of casualties from shellfire and sniping was inevitable.**

Aviators

Marine flying personnel wore the standard uniform; aviators were distinguished only by the wearing, just above the left breast pocket, of gold Navy pilot's wings, usually of pinback design or less commonly embroidered. In the air Marine pilots wore French or US leather or canvas coats and helmets. Spaulding was the most common US manufacturer of flying gear. One-piece French flying suits and thigh-length leather flight coats were the usual wear for aircrew, usually lined in wool, corduroy or fur. Marines first flew with the RAF, and some British gear was retained.

Since 1917, Navy flyers also wore the P1917 Marine officer uniforms and brown shoes, adding their naval shoulderboards and hats. The tradition of Navy flyers wearing 'greens' was to last until the 1980s, and brown shoes distinguish US Navy aviators to this day.

Marine Combat Uniforms

The P1917 Marine uniform had two strikes against it: its similarity to German *Feldgrau*, and Pershing's refusal to allow the AEF supply system to burden itself

with providing two separately coloured uniforms. By the time the Marines of the 2nd Division emerged from combat at Belleau Wood most had converted to the AEF drab uniforms. This gave the Marine troops what one veteran called a distinctively 'mottled appearance'. It is not an exaggeration to say that the Marines hated the M1912 Army/AEF uniform. It was uncomfortable and poorly made; but more importantly, by losing their distinctive P1917 uniform they were losing part of their identity. Marine officers generally retained their forest green uniforms (as did Ships' Company Marines of the North Sea Fleet), but the newly arriving 5th Brigade were issued AEF drab for everyday wear.

To keep their identity within the AEF, Marines commonly transferred their distinctive red-backed NCO stripes and Marine buttons to the replacement uniform. Additional signs of Marine tribal identification were the occasional display of the EGA insignia on helmets, pocket flaps and equipment. Late in the war the divisional insignia was also unofficially painted onto gas mask bags or other items. The most common appearance of the combat Marine was, nevertheless, as an anonymous AEF doughboy without any USMC distinctions at all.

ABOVE **A Marine of the 6th Regiment prepares to bring chow forward to the trenches: Verdun sector, March 1918.**

The Marine Brigade's 'mottled appearance' was maintained by the continued arrival at the front of replacements wearing the P1917 forest green uniform. Assistant Secretary of the Navy and future US President Franklin D.Roosevelt noted 'his' Marines' appearance during his September 1918 inspection of the Marine Brigade: '... Their own (forest green) having been worn out long ago ... It gives one a pretty good idea of the heavy casualties in the last fighting near Soissons' – the large number of replacements being easy to recognize in their darker P1917 Marine uniforms.

A future Commandant of the Marine Corps, then Lt.Cates, described his appearance in the trenches as follows:

'... Dirty, torn suit; wrapped putties; shoes that used to be boots, but are now cut off. Steel helmet, with a hole thru it and a big dent; pistol belt and suspenders; 1st aid package and cover; pistol and holster; canteen, cup and cover. Knapsack which holds toilet articles, maps, message book, extra cartridges, etc; field glasses and case; two extra pistol clips and case; German gasmask (which saved my life) and French gasmask (M2); big German Luger pistol and holster. Big musette bag with cigarettes, chocolate bars, magazine, writing paper, condiment can, malted milk tablets, comb, little clothes brush, alkaline tablets (for gas), and other junk. A blanket roll which contains a poncho, blanket, air-pillow, handkerchiefs, socks, underwear, etc.; and a German raincoat slung over my arm.'

Those Marines who served in **Russia** came off shipboard with standard issue P1917 uniforms and equipment. In winter their kit was sometimes supplemented by the issue of fur items and British cold weather parkas. These double-breasted parka/overcoats were of green

Two young Marines in P1917 uniforms are posed sharing a meal with their French allies, April 1918. Gasmasks, cartridge belts and a .45 pistol are evident on the left of the picture. US censors held up the release of this photo until after the Armistice – which seems inexplicable, unless it was felt that the folks back home would disapprove of their boys picking up degenerate foreign habits like drinking wine?

LEFT **March 1918: a Marine private serving as a VIP escort; like most Marines in the Verdun sector, he wears the P1917 forest green uniform with pointed breast pocket flaps. His mounted-pattern holster and British gasmask are clear here; the canteen cover is of an early Marine pattern, and his French M2 gasmask is still carried just behind his right hip.**

drab canvas, lined with sheepskin. Caps and mittens were commonly made of sealskin and muskrat; claw-buckle snow boots were also issued.

INSIGNIA AND DECORATIONS

Rank Insignia

Marine NCOs wore forest green chevrons on red backing patches on both arms of their P1917 coats. While many retained their chevrons and buttons when converting to the Army M1912 tunic, some inevitably came to use Army drab stripes. Early in 1918 the AEF authorized the wear of chevrons on the right sleeve only, and this soon became the standard. Late in the war the Marine Corps began to use the rank of private first class (PFC), but the prescribed crossed rifles insignia for this rank were not available in France until 1919.

The temporary titles of lance corporal or lance sergeant were also used during the war; these semi-official ranks were awarded as a sort of brevet to Marines who were serving as acting corporals or sergeants. The single stripe of lance corporal rank was formally authorized only for full dress use.

The rank of gunnery sergeant ('gunny') was created in 1898. By World War I it was used as the platoon sergeant rank, and was identified by crossed rifles and a flaming bomb. It originally denoted a shipboard sergeant proficient in smallarms, signalling and naval gunnery, and institution of the rank played a symbolic part in the Navy's internal struggle over whether the Marines were primarily to stay on board ship and serve as part of the vessel's guncrew. In 1900 half of the Corps was based on board ships; by 1914 only 5% were so based, marking a landward shift in the strategic direction of the Corps. Marines trained as naval gun pointers wore an embroidered drab deckgun insignia on their right cuff, and gun captains the Navy white embroidered cannon barrel.

A classic sketch by Lt.John W.Thomason of the 1/5th Marines showing a typical line officer in summer 1918, his cane, pistol and musette giving the outline characteristic of the first days of the Belleau Wood fighting that June. A company or battalion commander at that time would be known as 'the Skipper'. (SHSU)

Belleau Wood

Gen.Ludendorff's devastating offensive of 27 May 1918 hacked through the northern sector of the Western Front and nearly reached Paris in four days; the AEF 2nd Division, serving under French Sixth Army, were among the formations rushed to stem the tide, and on the night of 5 June the Marines of the 4th Bde were near Bouresches astride the Paris-Metz highway. Facing them across cornfields was Belleau Wood, held by about 1,200 German troops. The 5th Marines opened the assault at daybreak on 6 June, capturing a hill west of the woods at a cost of some 450 casualties. The brigade attack developed over the next week as the Marines pushed forward through Belleau Wood and Bouresches village, breaking the German third line by nightfall on the 12th, although much remained to be done in the northern half of the wood. The terrain was not the purely notional area of shell-shattered stumps which the term 'wood' usually meant on the Western Front, but was heavily wooded with trees in leaf, thick undergrowth and many rocky outcrops. Relieved by the US Army's 7th Infantry (5th Bde, 3rd Div) from 15 to 22 June, the Marines returned to the woods on the 23rd to find the front unchanged. A failed night attack was followed by heavy artillery preparation, and a final push on the 25th finally cleared the enemy out. As the US Marines' first pitched battle against enemy regular troops since 1814, Belleau Wood was a significant milestone in the Corps' history. The brigade's performance was highly praised by French and German observers alike.

These distinctions were earned by service with naval secondary batteries on shipboard, but were rarely displayed.

Officers pinned their rank insignia near the outboard end of the epaulettes; they sometimes removed them in combat to avoid standing out in a sniper's sights. The metal bars worn by lieutenants and captains were usually stamped to appear as though they were bullion-embroidered. Smaller paired rank insignia were worn on shirt collars. In mid-1918 the Army/Marine rank of second lieutenant was finally recognized by the authorizing for wear of gold lieutenant bars; these did reach France in late 1918.

All Marine officers wore mirrored (i.e. assymetric pairs of left and right) bronze EGA tunic collar devices; the anchors pointed inwards, and had no 'fouled' rope. Officers assigned as staff paymasters, quartermasters or aides-de-camp wore additional matching insignia outboard of their EGA collar devices.

For Marine officers arriving in France the dictates of local military fashion made walking sticks, trenchcoats and Sam Browne belts *de rigeur*. After Belleau Wood combat officers began to leave such items behind or mask them under foul weather coats; just as in the British Army, junior officers sometimes wore enlisted men's tunics and personal equipment to lower their profiles.

The Marines established the specialist rank of warrant officer in 1916. These men were mostly appointed from older veteran NCO ranks. They had special tasks such as administration (QM Clerk and, from 1919, Pay WO) or ordnance (Gunners). They were to be treated not as senior NCOs but as officers, though despite their service time they ranked junior to second lieutenants. Originally these hybrid Marines were directed to wear their subdued bursting bomb insignia on their

Marines in light combat order, awaiting the command to march. Under a magnifying glass Chauchat gunners can be made out at both ends of the platoon.

epaulettes. In France they took to wearing the bombs on their collars, and sometimes next to collar EGAs, staff officer style. A warrant officer's appearance was otherwise indistinguishable from a regular Marine officer.

Service and Wound Chevrons

AEF soldiers and officers were authorized to display overseas service and wound chevrons in September 1917. One (normally gold bullion) overseas chevron was worn above the left cuff for each six months' service in the theatre of operations; the most chevrons issued during the war was four. A wound chevron above the right cuff was awarded for each engagement in which a Marine was wounded or gassed. Both types were 2ins to 3ins wide, worn point down, the topmost chevron positioned 4ins to 5ins above the cuff. These stripes were sometimes worn on combat tunics. After the war they were worn on red backing on the P1917 Marine tunic.

LEFT **Marines with long packs and gasmasks mount up on French trucks. The drivers who took the Marines to Belleau Wood in June 1918 were Tonkinese (north Vietnamese) recruited into the French Colonial forces.**

RIGHT **Impression of a Chauchat gunner and ammunition bearers in action. Gunners found it was best to actually hold the magazine into this baulky weapon with the left hand to lessen the chances of jamming. Thomason consistently shows Marines wearing helmet EGAs in his drawings; this was artistic license, to show their Marine provenance. (SHSU)**

A small sky blue chevron worn point upwards was for service of less than six months overseas, and a silver chevron represented six months of home service, but neither type was commonly seen. A single small red chevron worn point up on the left arm represented a mustering-out soldier or Marine; ex-doughboys were authorized to continue to wear their uniforms for 90 days after discharge.

Four year service (re-enlistment) stripes were authorized for wear on both cuffs by all enlisted men. These were worn in full dress (in yellow silk on red) and on the forest green service uniform (green on red).

Collar Disks

The junior enlisted ranks had only the hat EGA and sometimes USMC buttons to identify them as Marines. Assistant Navy Secretary Roosevelt noticed this lack of insignia during his tour of inspection of the Marines in France. It was suggested that the Marine overcoat buttons be worn as collar devices (as they already were, unoffically, by some individuals). FDR authorized manufacture of Army-style bronze collar disks bearing the EGA minus fouled rope. Versions were made in France, the USA and later Germany. It appears likely that these disks were worn by some recently arrived replacements in time for the Meuse-Argonne offensive in November 1918.

Marines of the 77th (MG) Co. and some *poilus* await the Germans near Belleau Wood. Mostly Marine uniforms are evident; as the battle progressed, wear and tear forced Marines to change over completely to AEF drab. The sleeve insignia of the foreground men at second left and second right can just be made out – a gunnery sergeant and first sergeant respectively. This cumbersome but reliable and long-ranged French M1914 Hotchkiss was the standard equipment of USMC machine gun companies until the Armistice. (USNI)

These Marines of the 5th Regiment are happy to be marching out of Belleau Wood; note that the men in the foreground wear their raincoats as 'dusters'. It was commonly observed that the generals trucked you into the fighting, but you had to march out on your own.

Unit Patches

The 2nd Division's insignia was designed by a divisional truck unit in April 1918 as identification for use on vehicles. By August 1918 the division commander had tentatively authorized its use as a unit patch to be worn on the left shoulder: a white five-pointed star 3.5ins in diameter having the head of an American Indian facing forward embroidered in the centre. The Indian symbol was said to have been inspired by a US Indianhead gold coin (St Gaudin).

Over 40 manufacturing variations of this basic star and Indianhead design have been identified. Most of the patches worn in the field were home made from all sorts of materials. The basic Indianhead was not only embroidered or stamped, but also applied in ink or paint. Though rare, it appears that some French-made 2nd Division patches were worn prior to the Armistice, mainly by headquarters personnel. The 2nd Division does not seem to have received a full issue of Indianhead patches until early 1919. In the 1930s and 1940s any number of 'official' versions of the patch were to appear for use by veterans' groups.

The Indianhead and star motif was superimposed on cloth backgrounds of various shapes and colours to distinguish units of the division. The 5th Marine Regt used a square background and the 6th a squared diamond. The Regimental HQ, 1st, 2nd, 3rd Battalions and the MG Co. were identified by coloured backgrounds in black, red, yellow, blue and purple respectively. The lemon yellow of the 2nd Bn. was later changed to an orange yellow. Green backing represented supply units. The 6th Machinegun Battalion used a purple oblong oval background, and brigade headquarters a black oblong oval. Gen.Lejeune, as the divisional commander, wore a black shield-shaped background for divisional headquarters (and due to his features, he was commonly referred to as 'the Old Indian'). It is this format which is still used by the US Army as the shoulder sleeve insignia of the 2nd Division.

The basic star and Indianhead is known to have been hand-painted on some helmets and gas mask bags before the end of the war. Vehicles had the insignia painted on side panels, doors and tailgates by mid-1918.

The 2nd Division members of the 1919 AEF Composite Regiment occupation unit wore the star and Indianhead on a drab background. During the return voyage of the 2nd Division to the USA Indianhead patches were universally painted on the front of helmets, along with the mounting of EGAs.

In 1919 Marines of the 5th Brigade used a red disk with a white duckboard to mark their vehicles, in reference to their muddy duties at Camp Pontanezen, Brest. It is unclear if a duckboard shoulder patch was ever issued.

In mid-1919 a crimson patch bearing the EGA was issued in different shapes: square (11th Rgt), diamond (13th Rgt) or circular (HQ). The patch had a Roman numeral 'V' for the 5th Brigade in the centre, and this was later colour-coded to represent different units. Again, it is unclear to what extent this patch was ever issued.

The 1st Marine Aviation Force also authorized a patch based on the roundel and EGA symbol painted on their aircraft. This patch was worn – if at all – well after the Armistice.

A small battalion of Marines – the 15th – was stationed in northern Germany after the Armistice, and this unit became known as the 'Schleswig-Holstein' battalion. They had a red shield bearing the EGA painted on their helmet fronts.

Medals and Ribbons

During the war, long service Marines might be seen wearing the ribbons of the following campaign medals: Dewey Medal (Manila Bay); Sampson Medal (West Indies Naval); Spanish Campaign Medal; China Relief Medal (Boxer Rebellion); Philippine Campaign Medal (US Navy); Haitian Service Medal (US Navy) 1906/1917; Cuban Pacification Medal(US Navy); Nicaraguan Campaign Medal (US Navy); Mexican Service Medal (US Navy) 1902/1918; and the USMC Good Conduct Medal. Other medals for service prior to the war, including the Marine Corps Expeditionary Medal, were delayed in issue until after the Armistice.

The Medal of Honor (MoH) was the highest award for bravery that could be granted to a Marine. It came in an Army or a Navy version, the latter being suspended from the ribbon by an anchor. The recipient's act of bravery had to be witnessed and recommended by an officer. Of the AEF's 98 Medals of Honor, the Marines and sailors of the 2nd Division accounted for 18 awards, and Marine aviators received two more.

The Army's Distinguished Service Cross (DSC) was the next highest available award for bravery; Marines of the 4th Brigade received 500

DSCs during the war.

The Silver Star was awarded for bravery and mention in despatches; it was originally displayed as a $^3/_{16th}$-inch silver star attached to the World War I Victory Medal ribbon or ribbon bar. In 1932 the Silver Star was instituted as a decoration in its own right. The new Navy Cross was awarded retroactively to sailors and Marines just after the war for bravery or distinguished service, and was roughly the equivalent of the DSC. The Purple Heart for wounds was instituted after the war (1932).

The French *Croix de Guerre* was the most common foreign award bestowed on Marines, and its green and red striped ribbon with palms for additional awards was a common sight on veterans' tunics. A Verdun medal was awarded by the French shortly after the war to the 2nd and 3rd Divisions, for service in the Verdun/Chateau-Thierry sectors between March and July 1918.

More than 20 'bars' (clasps) could be awarded for wear with the rainbow-ribboned Victory Medal, most of them commemorating specific battles or sectors. When the ribbon is worn alone each clasp is represented by a bronze star. The 2nd Division would sport five battle bars: Aisne, Aisne-Marne (Soissons), St.Mihiel, Meuse-Argonne (Blanc Mont, Meuse-Argonne), and Defensive Sector. Marines of the 5th Brigade would wear a service bar 'France', which was later represented by a Maltese cross. For Russian service 'Russia' and 'Siberia' service bars were authorized; a 'Grand Fleet' bar marked Marine service in the North Sea Squadron; a 'West Indies' bar was issued for Caribbean service; and Marines serving elsewhere overseas wore the Victory Medal with an 'Overseas' bar.

Service ribbons, when worn, were placed above the left pocket. They could be worn four wide and were one inch high. They were placed either immediately above the top of the pocket flap, or sometimes two to three inches higher. Awards for bravery were worn at the top and to the centre of any ribbon display; campaign ribbons were worn in the date sequence of the service they represented.

Fourragère

The left shoulder lanyard in the green and red ribbon colours of the *Croix de Guerre* marked a collective French Army citation to the 4th Marine Brigade for valour and accomplishment in battle. Known in Marine parlance as the 'Pogey Rope' or 'Firehose', it was not officially worn by Marines of the brigade until two or three years after the Armistice. Each awardee was issued by Marine Corps HQ with a small wallet card as authorization for its wear. It is worn to this day by the 5th and 6th Marine Regiments as a remembrance.

Marksmanship Badges

These silvered badges were awarded in three descending grades: Expert, Sharpshooter and Marksman. The reverse was sometimes engraved with the owner's name. It was not unusual to see these badges proudly displayed on combat tunics or on shirts, by officers and enlisted men alike. They were worn just above the left pocket, below any medal ribbons. Similar Army issue badges were also worn. Monthly pro-pay of $2-5 'beer money' was granted for rifle qualification; a smaller pistol badge was also available. Approximately 70% of the Marine Corps scored as Marksmen or better. The 5th Marine Brigade, which sat out the war in the rear areas of France, had a marksmanship rate of 97%.

ABOVE **Gen.John A.Lejeune arrived in France after Belleau Wood. He soon proved himself at the head of the 4th Marine Brigade, and was given command of the crack 2nd Division by Pershing in August 1918. In this 1919 photo Maj.Gen.Lejeune wears the officer's P1897 hat, and the divisional patch on the black shield backing which originally identified only the headquarters.**

WEAPONS AND EQUIPMENT

M1903/M1917 Rifles

The M1903 Springfield .30 calibre rifle, with a five-round magazine, was almost universally carried by Marines in France. Light and handy at 8.5lbs, it was based on the German Mauser bolt action system, and its accuracy and reliability were much admired by the Corps. The issued .30in ammunition was the M1906 cartridge, commonly referred to as the '30-06'; this was a powerful round giving a flat trajectory, with a copper-jacketed, sharp-pointed 'spitzer' 150-grain bullet. The rifle was issued in blue/black gunmetal finish. The Springfield Arsenal was the primary manufacturer, and serial numbers below 1,050,000 could have seen war service. Rock Island Arsenal produced significantly fewer examples, and any serial number under 347,000 might have been in the trenches. The rifle had a metal hooded front sight cover which was removed in action; canvas three-snap action covers were available but rarely used.

The most commonly used sling was the M1907, made of russet brown leather with brass claw adjusters; this sling was specially developed for marksmens' use. The simpler cotton web Kerr sling was also issued for use with the '03'. A pull-through cleaning kit and brass oiler could be stored in the butt of the rifle; for every ten men a screw-together cleaning rod was issued in a special canvas case (the famous '3 in 1' oil was used to treat the Springfield and most other AEF weapons). The

1: Private, full dress, c.1914
2: Major, Staff; 5th Marine Regiment, USA, 1917
3: Sergeant, 6th Marine Regiment; France, 1917
4: Eagle, globe and anchor hat device

A

1: Corporal, 5th Marine Regiment; France, 1917
2: First Sergeant, 6th Machinegun Battalion; 2nd Division, Verdun, March 1918
3: Private, 6th Marine Regiment; 2nd Division, Verdun, spring 1918
4: USMC service button

B

5TH MARINE REGIMENT, BELLEAU WOOD, JUNE 1918:
1: Chauchat assistant gunner
2: Second Lieutenant
3: Corporal, Chauchat gunner

ST MIHIEL, SEPTEMBER 1918:
1: Gunnery Sergeant, 6th Marine Regiment
2: Private, 5th Marine Regiment
3: First Lieutenant, 6th Marine Regiment

D

1: Quartermaster Sergeant, 4th Marine Brigade, 1918
2: Pharmacist's Mate 2nd Class, US Navy; 4th Marine Brigade, 1918
3: Private, 5th Marine Regiment, summer 1918

CHAMPAGNE, OCTOBER 1918:
1: Major, 1st Battalion, 5th Marines; Blanc Mont
2: Runner, 5th Marines; Blanc Mont
3: Sergeant 1st Class, US Army Signal Corps; 2nd Division, St Étienne

F

ARGONNE, NOVEMBER 1918:
1: Grenadier, 4th Brigade
2: Assistant Browning Gunner, 5th Marines
3: Browning Gunner, 5th Marines

G

1

2

3

4

5

6

7

8

9

10

RIGHT **Like all Allied soldiers in France, these members of the 5th Marines band travel in a railway truck marked with its capacity – '40 men or 8 horses'. A postwar veterans' group took '40 & 8' as their name. Bandsmen served as stretcher bearers until it was noticed that too many of them were getting killed or wounded.**

Soissons & St Mihiel

In July 1918 the ruthless Gen.Mangin was given the AEF 1st and 2nd Divs to fight alongside his 1st Moroccan Div in XX Corps, French Tenth Army. The objective was the western face of the German salient south of Soissons. Maj.Gen.Harbord's 2nd Div had an exhausting night march up to their jumping-off line in heavy rain, but on 18 July the Marines moved off towards Vierzy behind a creeping barrage over easy ground. That evening they had to negotiate a deep morass and an embankment masking the town, but finally took it in some confusion, having advanced more than four miles in 24 hours – great progress by Western Front standards. The 9th saw them advance nearly to Tigny, but slow progress by the Moroccans exposed their left flank to counter-attacks by the reinforced enemy under skies dominated by German fighters; divisional casualties by now reached nearly 4,000, and they were relieved that night by the French 58th Colonial Division.

By late August the Allied armies were all making good progress in throwing back Ludendorff's last gamble. Pershing had been able to form the First American Army; and the AEF was given the task of reducing the St Mihiel salient south of Verdun, as a prelude to an ambitious advance through the Argonne forest to cut the Germans' vital supply railway from Strasbourg along the north bank of the Meuse.

The St Mihiel battle was the acid test of AEF staff work and preparation. The 2nd Div, camped in rain-swept woods for a week beforehand, attacked on 12 September 1918 on a one-kilometre front, as the middle of seven US divisions massed along the southern face of the salient. The Marines took heavy casualties in attacks on Mont Plaisir Farm, a fortified position of the Hindenburg Line; but the operation was an overall success, the Germans pulling back to the Michael Line with heavy loss in the last week of the month.

rifle took a 16in bright-bladed M1905 bayonet; for night patrols the blade was smoke-blackened, and later war production bayonets had dark blades. The leather-tipped canvas scabbard could be worn on either the side of the pack or on the belt.

As American arsenals were having problems keeping up with the demand for Springfields the British .303 P14 rifle – already in US production – was converted to take 30-06 and issued as the **M1917 Remington**, also known as the M1917 Enfield, Eddystone, M17 or P17. Common within the AEF, it was sometimes issued to Marine replacements and those serving outside France. Its sighting and handling were said by some to be superior to the Springfield 03. It took the M1917 Enfield bayonet and the M1907 or Kerr sling.

With telescopic sights mounted, 03s and a few P17s were used by Marines for sniping. The rifle took a Winchester A5 scope or, less frequently, the squat M1908/13 Warner & Swasey model; but some snipers preferred open sights. Both rifles also took specially modified French VB rifle grenade discharger cups.

M97/M1917 Trench Gun

Gen.Pershing authorized the purchase of the M97 Winchester 12-gauge pump action shotgun in 1917. This drafted riot gun was altered to accept the M1917 US Enfield bayonet. It carried six shells, each of which contained nine .00 buck (.32 cal) slugs. The shells, being made of cardboard with brass caps, tended to swell in the wet trenches; veterans would cycle old shells through the gun before action to make sure they would function. In the last weeks of the war full brass cartridges became available. Marines carried shotgun shells in their pockets or stuffed into M1910 rifle cartridge belts. A 32-round canvas pouch (M1918) was produced for the military, but it is unknown if these ever reached the trenches. It is possible that some civilian Mills web shotgun belts may have been used. With a 20-inch barrel the shotgun had limited range, but excelled in night actions, trench-clearing and as a weapon for guarding prisoners. The Germans hated it, and made formal protests to Geneva over its use. Interestingly, one of the original rationales for procuring these weapons was for shooting thrown German grenades out of the air. Marines received them in time for the St.Mihiel battle in August 1918. It is unlikely that the newer M1912 Winchester and M10 Remington pump shotguns reached France before the Armistice.

M1911/M1917 Pistol

Marine officers and many NCOs, runners and machine-gunners carried this stalwart semi-automatic pistol in action. It held seven .45 cal man-stopping bullets, and was admired by the Marines for its durability; this blued steel Colt pistol has continued in service for more than 80 years. The first magazines had a lanyard ring, as the authorities were sure that soldiers would loose them. It was intended to be carried with a round in the chamber 'cocked and locked'; it was, however, commonly carried with the hammer down. The pistol was carried in a 'US'-stamped brown leather M1912 flap holster on the right hip. This cavalry holster had an extended length or swivel feature. The rare Marine version had a stud to hold the flap open in lieu of a swivel, and was stamped 'USMC'. The fixed M1916 flap holster was more commonly used as the war went on. A two-magazine web pouch was mounted on the front of the pistol belt. A drab lanyard was available but rarely used.

The Marines' sister Army brigade commonly carried the six-shot .45 cal **M1917 revolver**; this was not a normal issue to the Marines, but was used to some extent. This blue-finished double-action pistol could take the new rimless .45 cartridge, held in the cylinder by a three-round half moon clip. The revolver was manufactured by Smith & Wesson and Colt ('new service') to different designs. Revolvers were carried in brown leather M1909/17 half flap holsters.

Several patterns of brass/steel **flare pistols** of British or French manufacture were used by the Marines, who referred vaguely to all these models by the British term 'Very pistols', after a famous make. The Remington Mk III became the most common US flaregun to reach the trenches.

Grenades

The Marines used a wide variety of French grenades and British Mills bombs, the former in distinct models termed offensive (OF) and defensive (DF) – the OF models were smooth-cased blast grenades, the DF segmented fragmentation grenades. Primitive gas and smoke grenades were also available.

As mentioned,the Marines also received the French Vivien-Bessieres (VB) rifle grenade system. The VB cup launcher (*tromblon*) was modified to fit on the muzzle of the 03 Springfield or the P17. The 50mm grenade, weighing about 3lbs, had a hole through the centre, and was discharged by firing a normal bulleted round; the bullet ignited the seven-second fuze as it passed through, and the gas pressure of the cartridge propelled the grenade out to a range of 200 yards. Signal rounds could also be fired from the VB cup. The launcher was carried in a leather and later a canvas bag on the belt.

Fighting knives

Two basic trench or fighting knives were issued to the Marines in 1918. Both these popular and fearsome-looking weapons had corrugated knuckleduster handguards so that they could be used for punching as well as stabbing. The M1917 had a darkened 9in triangular blade carried in a narrow leather and metal sheath similar to a bayonet scabbard; some of the later variations of the M1917/18 knife were issued in only limited numbers before the Armistice. The Mark I trench knife was developed by the AEF and initially made under French contract; its blade was marked with a prone lion *(au lion)*. It had a 6.5in double-edged blade, and its most distinctive feature was its all-bronze handle marked 'US 1918'. It was carried in a small black metal scabbard made to attach to the inside of the web pistol or cartridge belts.

The M1910/1917 Bolo was also commonly carried by Marines on a scale of one per squad. Its broad 10in blade was intended for general use, e.g. for cutting brush; machine gun teams used them to clear their fields of fire. The M1917 version differs only in the lack of a catch button for securing it in its canvas and leather scabbard. A rare metal scabbard was also used. The small M1910 hand axe was also issued to Marines in the trenches.

M1915 & M1918 CSRG (Chauchat) Automatic Rifles

The standard automatic rifle used by Marines in France throughout the war was the French CSRG or Chauchat, initially the M1915 model chambered for the big, sharply tapering French 8mm rifle round. This weapon proved to be controversial; its AEF nickname of 'Sho-Sho' was only the most printable among several alternatives. It had a reputation for frequent jamming and poor accuracy. A careful reading of its history shows it to have been a simple, cheap and relatively reliable automatic rifle, although quality control clearly suffered badly from the primitive production methods of the day. Its open bolt operation and exposed 20-round magazine did make it a magnet for dirt; the magazine was also frail and often caused feed problems; the long travel of the bolt did not make for either accuracy or reliable recycling in automatic fire; and an inexperienced gunner putting his face near the rear of the action would receive a distinctive Chauchat bruise on his right cheek (the *poilus* called it 'the smack'). The gun weighed 22lbs loaded and had a rate of fire of

The US Army's 2nd Engineers and 12th Field Artillery worked closely with the Marine Brigade within the 2nd Division, and the leathernecks considered them honorary Marines. In this Thomason sketch these two combat engineers are distinguished from any other doughboys only by their shovel and pick. (SHSU)

US Army troops of the 23rd Infantry, 2nd Division operate a 37mm gun in this classic Great War photo, taken at St Mihiel in September 1918. The gunners' packs are lightly stowed for combat, and the first aid pouch is worn at the back so as to be out of the way.

250rpm; it could be fired semi- or fully automatic. It was designed to offer assault infantry the support of 'walking fire', and it could be fired from the hip on the move, if with some difficulty. Some Marines claimed that it was manufactured out of old sardine cans. Marine Lt.Sam Meeks said of it: 'That damn Chauchat, it was a lousy weapon in many ways, but it was another dirt absorber. It was not very accurate, but it usually worked, and this is a great asset in the type of combat we were in. You could use it like a hose.'

A later M1918 version, incompetently redesigned to take the US .30-06 cartridge, was even worse, and has in part been responsible for the Chauchat's bad overall reputation. The AEF Marines received only the 8mm version; carefully handled, it served them well enough. Sixteen Chauchats were issued to each company; a gun team consisted of the gunner and two ammo-carriers, who each carried a special French haversack holding four magazines. A full canvas and leather carrying case was available for this weapon. The Chauchat was to have no competitors until the arrival of the 'light Browning'.

Browning Automatic Rifle

The M1918 .30 cal light Browning was first 'obtained' by Marines from the 36th (Texas) Division during the October 1918 Blanc Mont offensive, but these had to be returned to the Texans before the Marines were allowed to withdraw from the sector. It could be fired at 500rpm in fully or semi-automatic mode, and compared with the Chauchat its quality of manufacture was of an entirely different order. With a 20-round magazine it weighed just 17lbs; it had an extra long three-claw brown leather sling, but at this date no bipod. The BAR (a postwar

Champagne: Blanc Mont

At the beginning of October the 2nd Div was attached to Gen.Gouraud's French Fourth Army for an attack northwards, while the American First Army fought east of them in the Argonne. Their objective was the dominating Blanc Mont ridge between Sommepy and St Étienne in Champagne. They attacked on 3 October over the shell-churned chalk: an officer of the 1/5th Marines called it 'a great white sea that has been dead and accursed through all time'. The 4th Bde assaulted the left flank of the ridge with the Army's 3rd Bde on their right. Both made spectacular progress, but the French on their flanks could not keep up; the doughboys spent the night in two separate salients on the ridge, under fire from three sides. They linked up on the 4th, and held a 500-yard-wide salient pushing a mile and a half into the German lines until relieved late on the 5th. On 6 October they forced their way onwards towards St Étienne-à-Arnes. When they were within a thousand yards of the objective the 4th Bde were heavily counter-attacked in the exposed left flank. Maj.Hamilton's 1/5th Marines swung half left and advanced without artillery support, driving the Germans back before turning again to resume the yard-by-yard advance on the town. Two companies of the 6th Marines finally broke into St Étienne on 8 October, and further enemy counter-attacks were held off until they were relieved by 71st Bde from 36th Div. 2nd Div losses in this battle were just under 5,000 men – 726 killed, 3,662 wounded and 585 missing. The Allied commander-in-chief Marshal Foch said of the battle that it was 'the greatest single achievement' of the operations in Champagne.

term) proved to be an outstanding weapon, and would remain in the US inventory until the late 1960s. A limited number were formally issued to the Marine Brigade in late October, in time for the Meuse-Argonne offensive.

Hotchkiss and Browning Machine Guns

Unfortunately, the Marines were forced to hand over their fine Lewis man-portable light machine guns to the Air Service upon arrival in France. In their stead they were issued – in common with the other units of the 2nd Division – with AEF standard French M1914 8mm Hotchkiss medium machine guns. These were found fairly reliable and hard-hitting, but Marines complained about their weight and clumsiness; mules and carts were normally used to transport this heavy weapon, which weighed more than 100lbs with its tripod mount. The air-cooled Hotchkiss was fed by metal stripper trays of 24 or 30 cartridges, and had a cyclic rate of about 500 rounds per minute.

The Marines received the new belt-fed Browning M1917 machine gun just after the Armistice. This water-cooled weapon, manufactured in .30-06 by Colt, Westinghouse and Remington, was arguably the best of its type in the war, and weighed a 'light' 37lbs with a full water jacket. The belt-fed M1917 and the BAR were released to American forces in large numbers on the eve of the Meuse-Argonne offensive of October-November 1918; Pershing held up the issue of both weapons to prevent the Germans from capturing and copying them. Additionally, he hoped the surprise effect would be heightened by using them in mass.

M1916 37mm Gun

At the regimental and brigade level the M1916 37mm direct fire gun (the 1-pounder, or 'toy gun') was used by the Marines. This single-shot French weapon – the same as mounted in the FT.17 Renault tank – fired a small explosive shell which would pierce ¾in of armour plate at 2,500 yards, and it proved to be especially effective at suppressing snipers and machine guns. A canister round holding 32 slugs could also be used. A rate of fire of 20 rounds a minute could be maintained by a practised three-man crew. It was provided with a gunshield, but this was rarely seen in the field.

Mortars

The Marines used the British 3in Stokes mortar, at a scale of six per regiment. The Stokes could throw a 10lb bomb out to 1,200 yards. All other artillery support in the 2nd Division was provided by Army 75mm and 155mm howitzers, and a battery of 6in heavy mortars.

Vehicles

The Marines were authorized no vehicles for their units headed for France. One Model T Ford truck was donated to the 6th Marines by a Mrs Elizabeth Pearce, which would be used to run ammunition and supplies into Belleau Wood. Nicknamed 'Tin Lizzie', the Ford was all but wrecked, but won for its passengers the Distinguished Service Cross for this exploit. Horses, mules and donkeys were used by Marines for hauling machine guns and supplies; pigeons were used to carry messages from the trenches to headquarters.

$187 Harley-Davidson, Excelsior and Cleveland motorcycles, some with sidecars, were used as courier vehicles. French- and US Army- crewed tanks of French manufacture were used in supporting Marine attacks.

WEB GEAR AND EQUIPMENT

The basic M1910 canvas webbing accoutrements were used throughout the war by the Marines. The webbing made prior to 1917 was secured with metal snap fasteners impressed with the National Eagle, or Marine Corps button snaps. The 'lift-the-dot' (LTD) fastener for webbing was used for most gear produced during the war; this comprises a stud and a 'doughnut collar' snap better able to function in the mud.

Webbing was ink-stamped by the manufacturer 'US', although some 'USMC'-stamped gear was also produced. Field gear was produced by several private manufacturers. The Mills Equipment Company was the designer as well as a major manufacturer; Russell was another large-scale wartime producer, as was the government's Rock Island Arsenal (RIA). Webbing was normally khaki coloured, but some of the early Marine webbing was olive green or 'blancoed' green with a scrubbed-on preservative preparation.

The M1910 **cartridge belt** had two five-pocket sections, each pocket holding two five-round brass stripper clips; the rear clip was stowed with the bullets pointing downwards, and the front clip pointing upwards. An internal snap strap inside the pocket held the front clip in place when the pocket was left open. Belts produced prior to 1917 had puckered or gathered pouch bottoms and snap closures. The puckers were designed to restrain the pointed M1906 bullets. By 1918 most belts had LTD fasteners and had lost this pucker. Various items such as canteens, bayonets and aid pouches were hung by hooks from the many black metal eyelets along the edge of the M1910 belt.

Cavalry pattern M1910 cartridge belts were also used by the Marines and can be identified by one pouch less on the right front. This was commonly replaced with a two-magazine pistol pouch.

By 1917 much of the M1910 gear was being produced in canvas instead of cotton webbing; this wartime canvas gear is sometimes referred to as 'M1918 equipment' by collectors. Though the M1910 gear was the most commonly used by Marines, earlier one-piece M1903/07 nine-pocket web cartridge belts were also to be seen. Individual Marines marked the inside of cartridge belts with their name using ink stamps. Additional expendable six-pocket (60-round) cloth bandoleers were issued to riflemen as they went forward into the line. These were lined with cardboard, as the pointed M1906 bullet would otherwise push its way through the light cloth. A knot was tied in the tape sling to adjust it.

The 'light Browning' or **BAR gunner's M1918 magazine carrier belt** appeared in several variations. The first pattern had a two-clip pistol ammo pouch and two BAR magazine pouches on the right side and three BAR pockets on the left. The second and more common gunner's belt had a horizontal metal cup on the right side, to hold the braced butt of the Browning while firing from the hip. The assistant gunner's belt had two BAR pockets on each side, plus two regular rifle pockets on each side of the front buckle. A model with six BAR pockets was also used. A three-pocket bandoleer was made, but it is unclear if these reached the trenches. Each Browning ammo pouch held two 20-round magazines.

The web **M1912 pistol belt** was intended for Marines who had no need to carry a rifle cartridge belt. Like the latter, the pistol belt had numerous metal eyelets for mounting associated equipment items. This belt could have attached to it the pistol holster, canteen, magazine pouch and first aid pouch as well as the backpack. Officers, senior NCOs, machinegunners and hospital corpsmen commonly used this belt.

When available, the **M1907 web suspenders** could be worn with either belt to help distribute the weight. It was intended,however, for the **M1910 haversack** (backpack) to be worn in conjunction with these belts and to serve that purpose. The overly complex M1910 haversack was an awkward carry when fully loaded. It could only be worn with its straps attached to the cartridge or pistol belt, since it lacked a separate set of shoulder straps. For the assault it was obviously packed much lighter and smaller. Unfortunately, to get something out of the pack it had to be fully opened.

A **blanket** could be carried rolled and attached to the bottom of the pack, making it a 'long pack'. Marines carried both Army drab and Marine issue green wool blankets. Marine blankets had a woven 'US' in the centre. In 1918 the AEF began to carry a blanket rolled in a shelter half canvas, 'horseshoe style' around the outside of the pack.

Bayonets were carried on the left side of the pack or belt. The

Private John Kelly of the 6th Marines receives the Medal of Honor from Gen.Pershing in 1919. Kelly wears the Army M1917 uniform with 2nd Division shoulder patch but without collar disks, a drab overseas hat with EGA device, and a stripped pistol belt.

scabbards were of rawhide-covered wood with an outer sheath of khaki web and a russet leather tip. The T-handle **entrenching shovel** and the **mess kit** both had canvas covers and attached to the rear centre of the pack; it was not uncommon for Marines to have these two items shot up while laying prone under fire. A small two-piece M1910 pick/mattock set could also be carried.

Officers used haversacks of several patterns, generically called by the French term *musette*. They sometimes carried their effects rolled into a blanket/poncho 'Rebel roll' worn bandoleer style, as stipulated in prewar regulations. Besides a haversack, an officer might carry a mapcase, a compass and binoculars.

Medical corpsmen and Chauchat teams carried special haversacks. **Grenades** were carried in pockets, haversacks, sandbags or canvas buckets. A purpose-made 11-pocket carrying 'vest' or apron with plain snap fasteners was issued by mid-1918 for both hand and rifle grenades; it was commonly worn over one hip with a tied loop over the wearer's opposite shoulder. The special M1914 medical belt with its eight large pockets was also pressed into service to carry grenades.

The canvas **shelter half** was usually carried wrapped around a blanket or folded within the pack. As with most 'dog' tents, this shelter half buttoned together with a partner's half to form a low two-man tent. Four wooden tent pegs, rope, and a three-piece metal-jointed wooden tent pole were included in the set. A poncho or raincoat could be thrown over the open end to extend and close the tent.

The **M1910 aid pouch** was a plain-snap webbing or canvas pocket which held a wound bandage; a USN/Marine pattern pouch slightly bigger than the M1910 was also used. The bandage was contained in a brass case sealed with lead which could be ripped open by a pull tab. Later dressings were wrapped in thin waterproof canvas.

The **M1910 canteen** was aluminum and held one quart; the date of manufacture and the company name are usually found marked on the side. The lower half of the canteen fitted inside the canteen cup carried in the bottom of the insulated cover; the cup had the date and manufacturer stamped on the bottom. After Belleau Wood it was not uncommon for Marines to carry two canteens into action.

The **M1908 wirecutters** were carried on the belt in a LTD open-top case. These were found to have a problem cutting the German manganese barbed wire, and the large French M1918 cutters in a leather belt carrier were also issued.

Marines used the voluminous seabag to carry the rest of their clothing and gear, normally stamped with the owner's name. This item was left behind when they went to the front. The modern equivalent (dufflebag) is still used today by US troops. Marines commonly referred to large artillery shells as 'seabags'.

Gasmasks

The Marines were initially issued the French M2 gasmask, a simple design made from a resin-impregnated canvas cloth; the filter was integral to the mask, so no hose or separate container were required. It was carried in a semicircular-shaped canvas satchel.

When the British small box respirator (SBR) – reportedly developed from a US ore-miner's protective mask – was issued to the Marines in early 1918, the M2 was retained and carried as a back-up. The canvas mask of the SBR had an integral noseclip and 'snorkel' mouthpiece, which connected by a corrugated hose to a tin filter canister carried in a canvas satchel. This was worn slung like a haversack when out of the line, and in the 'ready' position around the neck to hang on the chest when in action; a length of whipcord attached to D-rings was passed around the wearer's back and tied off to prevent the bag bouncing around when in movement.

The American CE ('corrected English') box respirator became available in mid-1918. This was a slightly improved copy of the SBR. It had a large number stamped on the nose of the mask to show size; a small card was kept with the bag, recording that mask's use history. The bag was similar to the British one except for lift-the-dot snaps on the flap replacing the British pebble-finish brass snaps, and a metal claw fitting to shorten the sling and hold the bag in the high 'ready' position.

Col.Catlin described wearing the mask: 'A hot and stifling thing that seems to impede the faculties ... Imagine fighting with a clothespin on your nose and a bag over your mouth and you may be able to get some notion of what a gas mask is like.'

These masks did not protect the user from the chemical burns which mustard gas caused on exposed skin. Uniforms could become so heavily impregnated with chemicals as to require quick disposal.

Miscellaneous items

Identity tags These aluminum 'dogtags' were issued two per man. They were hung on a metal cable covered in cloth and worn around the neck. Upon death, one disk was left with the body and the other was removed and handed in to unit headquarters. The disk was stamped with the Marine's name, date of enlistment and 'USMC' on one side, and on the other his AEF serial number. Officers' tags were stamped with their rank. By the end of the war the individual's religion was also stamped on the disk (C, P or H for Catholic, Protestant or Hebrew). The earliest tags, issued from August 1917, were square; one disc and one square tag were issued from February 1918, and both tags were circular by mid-1918. Privately purchased bracelets with names engraved were also worn; and photo identity cards were used within the AEF by officers.

Rations Cook wagons ('galleys') prepared hot food for the Marines

when possible. This 'hot chow' would be carried up to the company positions in thermal *marmite* containers. Two-day reserve field rations issued for carrying by the Marines were mostly from US sources. Food in the trenches consisted of canned hash ('Bill' or 'Willie', in reference to the Kaiser), canned salmon or sardines ('goldfish'), salt pork ('sowbelly'), hard bread ('crackers'), canned tomatoes, pork & beans ('repeaters'), bacon, jam, and instant coffee. Most disliked was the canned beef and carrot stew provided by the French, of Argentine or Madagascan origin; and canned meat of any kind was known as 'monkey' (as in French army slang) or 'kangaroo'. Meat stews were called 'slum'. One delicacy was the 'trench doughnut'; this was bread dough fried in bacon fat and covered with sugar. The Civil War favorite of crumbled crackers in bacon grease ('skillygalee') was rediscovered by Marines at Belleau Wood. An emergency ration can of meat, bread and chocolate was also carried but was not to be consumed unless authorized by an officer. Tobacco (Bull Durham), cigarettes and candy were issued free. Jellied gasoline or Sterno ('canned heat') was issued to the Marines for smokeless cooking fires; artillery guncotton was also used for the same purpose.

Mess gear The two-piece M1910 mess kit was found to be too shallow and a deeper-dish M1918 version was rapidly issued. The plates and handle could be interconnected and balanced so as to be held in one hand. In a pinch, the pan would be used as a entrenching tool. Mess kits were sometimes artistically engraved by their owners with name, unit and EGA, as well as battle honours. The 'US'-stamped spoon and fork were tin-plated and the knife had an aluminum handle; 'USMC'-stamped silverware also exists. Mess gear also included the M1916 bacon can and the double-ended M1910 condiment can.

1917 Pay scale Marine privates were paid little more than their American Civil War predecessors. Additional rates were paid to specialists such as cooks, clerks, gun pointers and signal personnel, and also

Visible in this candid 1919 photo of a work detail of the 80th Co., 2/6th Marines, are a variety of uniform details. They all wear Army drab, and most display the EGA on their overseas hats. Notice the Marine shirt and German belt (third man from left), and sleeveless pullover sweater (seventh from left).

for rifle qualification. Interestingly, 20 cents per month was deducted for medical care. Monthly base pay was as follows:

Private	$15
PFC	$18
Corporal	$21
Sergeant	$30
SgtMaj, 1st Sgt, QM Sgt, Gny Sgt	$45
2nd Lt	$141

FURTHER READING

Asprey, R., *At Belleau Woods* (1965)
Berry, H., *Make The Kaiser Dance* (1978)
Brannen, C., *Over There* (1996)
Heinl, R., S*oldiers of the Sea* (1960)
Mackin, E., *Suddenly We Didn't Want to Die* (1993)
Stallings, L., *Doughboys* (1965)
Thomason, J., *Fix Bayonets* (1929)

The workhorse of the Marine squadrons in France was the British-designed, American-built de Havilland DH-4, a two-seat light bomber and observation aircraft which could carry 500lbs of bombs and was powered by a 400hp American Liberty engine. It had an adequate if unspectacular performance, with a top speed of 125mph and a ceiling of 17,000 feet. Fuel storage between the cockpits helped earn it the unlovely nickname of 'the flaming coffin'. Armament was two forward-firing Marlin machine guns and single or twin Lewis MGs for the rear cockpit gunner. The Marine force had 16 DH-4s and eventually 20 of the superior DH-9As divided between their four squadrons. Marines flew the Curtiss JN-4B 'Jenny' during training in the USA.

THE PLATES

A1 Private, full dress, c.1914

The Marines have only gradually changed their full dress from the Civil War until the present day, and it has always retained its essential characteristics: a long dark blue tunic piped with red, and light blue trousers. This private wears the P1912 uniform; a service stripe marks over six years' service with the Corps, and he wears the ribbon of the Good Conduct Medal. NCOs were distinguished by sleeve chevrons and leg stripes; they carried swords instead of rifles, and their sword belt buckle had an embossed eagle motif. Marines always wore russet brown footwear except when in full dress, when black shoes were worn.

A2 Major, Staff; 5th Marine Regiment, USA, 1917

A quartermaster working on the dockside as the 5th Marines embark in the USA, in the P1912 tropical uniform as usually worn in the Caribbean or the Pacific. Upon arrival in France all Marines changed over to the forest green service uniform. On his collar he displays the dual staff and EGA insignia. A small

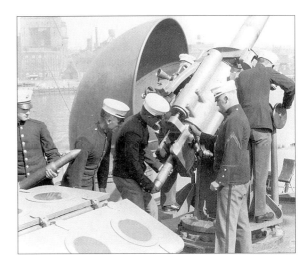

Marines in blues man a 5in gun on the USS *Pennsylvania*. Note the service stripe on the forearm of the corporal in the foreground, and his leg stripe. White hat covers are worn for summer service.

ABOVE **Gny.Sgt.Dan Daly had previously won two Medals of Honor (for the Boxer Rebellion and the Haiti operations) before 1914; he went on to win the DSC at Belleau Wood. He appears here in dress blue uniform, c.1919; note the anchor suspenders of the naval Medal of Honor. It was Gunny Daly who was reputed to have shouted during the initial assault on Belleau Wood, 'Come on you sons-of-bitches – do you want to live forever?' This 'Marine's Marine' was just 5ft 6ins tall and weighed in at 132lbs. He died in retirement at the age of 63.**

percentage of Marine officers were permanent members of the staff, serving only in staff and support echelons; they were assigned and promoted separately from Marine line officers. This officer's ribbons are for the Nicaraguan Campaign and Cuban Pacification medals. The major's .45 automatic is carried in a rare USMC P1912 holster.

A3 Sergeant, 6th Marine Regiment; France, 1917

This young sergeant is ready to march away from the docks after disembarkation at St Nazaire. His Marine P1917 uniform is easily distinguished from US Army drab by its forest green colour and the breast pocket pleats. A helmet and gasmask will soon be added to his burden. He has the USMC snap canteen cover, and may well be wearing the early P1903/07 cartridge belt. His long pack has his blanket roll in the bottom portion. The mess kit sits in a canvas pouch on the back of the pack, and his bayonet on the off side. Many junior NCOs were also issued .45 pistols as well as the 1903 Springfield rifle.

A4 Eagle, globe and anchor hat device

This insignia began to be worn by the US Marines just after the Civil War. This 1.5in version was worn on campaign hats and overseas caps by all Marines. The smaller collar version, worn by officers only, had no rope 'fouling' the anchor.

B1 Corporal, 5th Marine Regiment; France, 1917

Americans were commonly called 'Sammies' by the Allies when they first arrived in France, in reference to Uncle Sam. Soldiers hated this nickname, and it gradually passed out of use. This Sammy is a Marine on pass, in what the British would call walking-out dress. A dark brown leather belt was sometimes worn with this outfit. His corporal's chevrons are worn on both sleeves, and he displays the Sharpshooter's badge over his left breast pocket. By early 1918 the campaign hat would be traded for a drab Army overseas hat, and puttees would be worn.

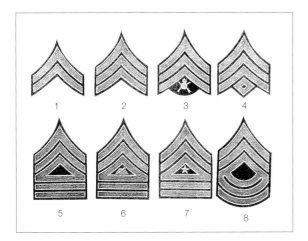

NCO sleeve insignia of rank: (1) Corporal, (2) Sergeant, (3) Gunnery Sergeant, (4) First Sergeant, (5) Quartermaster Sergeant, (6) Pay QM Sergeant, (7) Drum Major, (8) Sergeant Major.

B2 First Sergeant, 6th Machinegun Battalion; 2nd Division, Verdun, March 1918

The 4th (Marine) Brigade of the 2nd Division first deployed to the trenches on 17 March (St Patrick's Day) near Verdun. This first sergeant, like the vast majority of Marines, is still wearing his P1917 uniform; the AEF (Army) M1917 drab uniforms were available but were not generally worn. His sleeve shows three service stripes (these were rarely worn). Visible on his belt is the M1910 bolo, used by MG units clear fields of fire. Obscured here on his right hip is a .45 pistol. His British SBR gasmask satchel is worn reversed – i.e. with its front face to the chest – in the ready position. The first sergeant ('top kick') is the senior NCO in his company.

B3 Private, 6th Marine Regiment; 2nd Division, Verdun, spring 1918

This hungry Marine carries the French issue ammunition haversack for the CSRG (Chauchat) automatic rifle, holding four magazines with a weight of over 8lbs; he also has a French 2-litre water canteen. He is without his backpack, and so wears the bayonet scabbard hooked to his cartridge belt. This private still has prewar US boots, but will soon have them replaced with hobnailed French or British issue or US M1917/18 'Pershing' boots. His British gasmask is worn high ready for instant use in case of a gas alarm. Note his exposed shirt collar, commonly worn in this manner to prevent the tunic collar from chafing.

B4 USMC service button

The Marine Corps service button bearing the EGA motif has remained essentially unchanged since 1804. It was worn in a dark bronze on all uniforms except dress blues, where it was worn in bright brass. It was issued in three sizes; ⁵⁄₈in for pockets, ⁷⁄₈in for tunics, and 1in for overcoats.

Plate C: 5th Marine Regiment, Belleau Wood, June 1918:

C1 Chauchat assistant gunner

This private wears the early P1904/07 cartridge belt with Marine buttonsnap pouches. His clothing is the Marine issue wool shirt and trousers; this summer battle saw many Americans fighting in shirtsleeves. The Marine shirt's pointed pocket flaps were its most distinctive feature; it appears to be cut pullover style, but in fact the front opening is full length. His British and French gasmask bags sit at his feet; a French issue Chauchat ammunition haversack hangs on his left hip – the magazine of the Chauchat was commonly called a 'clip' by Marines. His pack and bayonet scabbard have been left in a nearby foxhole. Legend has it that the term 'foxhole' was actually coined at Belleau Wood to describe a shallow one- or two-man fighting position.

C2 Second Lieutenant

Though enlisted Marines were beginning to change to the AEF drab uniform, officers continued to wear their forest green uniforms. This lieutenant's tunic and breeches are made of a lighter wearing barathea material rather than wool. He has no rank insignia; the gold bar for second lieutenant has yet to be authorized, but his status is immediately visible from his Sam Browne and collar EGAs. A signal whistle and chain hang from his right pocket. He is armed with a .45 pistol in a M1912 cavalry pattern holster, and his British gasmask is worn slung haversack style. After a 20-day battle for Belleau Wood, a Marine officer was able to report 'Woods now US Marine Corps' entirely'.

C3 Corporal, Chauchat gunner

After the initial fighting in Belleau Wood the Marine Brigade was withdrawn for a short rest (15-22 June). During the lull Marines in large numbers changed over to AEF drab uniforms. This corporal wears the Army issue shirt as well as trousers. His CSRG automatic rifle weighs about 21lbs loaded; the magazine, whose open side exposed it to fouling,

ABOVE **Officer insignia of rank (epaulette) and department (collar).**

ABOVE **This gunnery sergeant wears the Army uniform, but is identified as a Marine by his rank stripes (just visible on his right sleeve), and the EGA badge on the left front of his overseas hat. He also shows an overseas stripe on his left forearm (more than six months' service in theatre), two medal ribbons and a marksmanship badge over his left pocket.**

had a 20-round capacity (although its weak spring exacerbated the weapon's feed problems if it was fully loaded). His gasmasks are not readily visible here.

Plate D: St Mihiel, September 1918:

D1 Gunnery Sergeant, 6th Marine Regiment

This 'gunny' has armed himself with the newly-issued Winchester M97 shotgun; he might also have a .45 on his hip, but not in this case. He wears the standard AEF (Army) drab uniform with web gear and pack. His helmet, boots and gasmask are still of British manufacture. He wears rank stripes on his right sleeve only. Gunnery sergeant was the senior NCO in a Marine platoon, and he would also normally act as the company first sergeant in the trenches – the actual first sergeant would often be absent for long periods, arranging logistics and support for his company.

D2 Private, 5th Marine Regiment

This Marine clothed in Army drab loads his '03' from a five-round stripper clip; he wears nothing identifying him as a Marine except his dogtags. His backpack is lightly loaded, as was normal in the assault. His bayonet is still in its pack-mounted scabbard. A souvenir German belt is just visible among his gear, as is a disposable 50-round cotton bandoleer of rifle ammunition; if he is carrying a grenade, it is probably stuffed into a coat pocket. His Army breeches are laced tight just below the knees. The US-made bag for the CE gasmask – readily identified by the lift-the-dot fasteners – is in the ready position.

D3 First Lieutenant, 6th Marine Regiment

The wearing of enlisted men's uniforms and equipment by junior officers was not uncommon in the British or American armies. This expedient helped their expensive privately tailored uniforms to last longer if spared the rigours of the trenches; more importantly, it lowered the casualty rates among junior leaders. Surprisingly, this first lieutenant ('1st Lewis') still wears silver bars on his Army drab tunic epaulettes. An officer's haversack or musette hangs on his right hip. His 03 rifle has the canvas Kerr sling which first began to appear that summer in place of the leather pattern. A pack and US gasmask bag are also worn by this front line leader.

E1 Quartermaster Sergeant, 4th Marine Brigade, 1918

This quartermaster wears the standard Army/AEF drab uniform and puttees. His red-backed NCO stripes and the EGA on his M1916 holster mark him as a Marine. EGAs were also worn unofficially on helmets, gasmask bags and tunic pocket flaps, and Marine pattern buttons might also be sewn on to the tunic, to emphasise the identity of a Marine in the huge AEF. The canteen cup is of a pattern still in use today. His pistol belt supports a .45 holster, first aid pouch and canteen. On the front offside would be a double magazine pouch for his pistol.

E2 Pharmacist's Mate 2nd Class, US Navy; 4th Marine Brigade, 1918

This sailor's parent service is also hidden under the Army drab uniform, and only his rank patch identifies him as Navy. He wears it on the right arm in violation of Navy regulations but in obedience to AEF regulations; most AEF medical corpsmen wore rank on the left, under the red cross brassard. He has an M1910 eagle snap ten-pocket medical belt with M1907 suspenders, supporting a flashlight on the front and probably two canteens on the rear. In his left hand he carries here a medical haversack and instrument roll, and his US gasmask bag hangs on his hip while out of the line. A section of two to five Hospital Corpsmen were assigned to each line company, a Pharmacist's Mate serving as the senior rating. In World War I doughboys generally shouted for 'first aid' when they needed medical assistance; Marines shouted for a 'corpsman' in World War II. Of the 350 Hospital

ABOVE **A Corpsman treats the foot of a Marine corporal; both wear Marine P1917 uniforms, and the former still has leggings. Just visible is the medic's left sleeve badge – a plain red cross without stripes – identifying him as an Apprentice Hospital Corpsman. Note the corporal's US wirecutters and .45 pistol slung on the right hip; and his interesting headgear – the crown of a cut-down campaign hat.**

Corpsmen eventually assigned to the 2nd Division, 164 were killed, wounded or captured.

E3 Private, 5th Marine Regiment, summer 1918

Replacements arriving with the Marine Brigade from the USA still wore the P1917 forest green uniform, and were known as 'greenies'. This wounded Marine's marksmanship badge and 'dogtags' are visible. He has been tagged by the corpsman who first reached him, with a label showing his injury and treatment; if he were a gas casualty he would also have a large 'X' inked on his forehead. His arm sling is a Navy kerchief. This wound will earn him the right to display a small gold chevron on the right cuff of his tunic – the Purple Heart medal for wounds received in battle was only (re)instituted in 1932.

In the background is a Ford ambulance marked with the 2nd Division insignia; small, handy and durable, these workhorse vehicles served the Allies well as forward ambulances. Further to the rear the wounded would be transferred to larger vehicles, and finally to trains.

Plate F: Champagne, October 1918:

F1 Major, 1st Battalion, 5th Marines; Blanc Mont

This Marine's boots, mapcase, cane and trenchcoat all mark him out as an officer. He wears the P1917 forest green wool uniform under the trenchcoat. The high, laced field or 'aviator's' boots were quite widely worn, though not universally popular. His early pistol magazine pouch has snap buttons. He wears a US gasmask bag in the hooked-up

or ready position. As a major he commands a 1,000-man battalion and captains command his four companies; by the end of the assault on Blanc Mont ridge on 3 October and the immediate push on to capture St Étienne on the 4th to 8th, it was common for second lieutenants or even NCOs to be leading depleted companies out of the line.

F2 Runner, 5th Marines; Blanc Mont

This private is marked as a battalion runner ('dog robber') by his red brassard, which allowed him free movement throughout the divisional area. (Unfortunately it also marked his dead body as worth searching for undelivered messages.) A blue brassard was used by signalmen and a black 'MP' brassard by the Military Police. This runner is lightly equipped so as to be unencumbered, carrying only a gasmask, pistol and fighting knife. He wears the standard Army/AEF M1917 overcoat but in this case cut short for ease of movement and to keep its skirts out of the mud, which could add many pounds to its weight. Most US officers were not allowed soldier servants or batmen; runners, unit buglers and drivers were often employed in this capacity to some degree (this is still the case today in the US military).

F3 Sergeant 1st Class, US Army Signal Corps; 2nd Division, St Étienne, October 1918

More than half of the 2nd Division consisted of US Army units, and all divisional support units were Army except for some US Navy medical personnel. Only a limited number of Marines were trained to act as signalers, and these provided most of the communications within the 4th Brigade. This Army signalman tests the phone wires to a Marine 'post of command' (PC). He wears AEF drab with collar disks and NCO chevrons on his right sleeve only; his corps is identified by crossed flag motifs on the disks and his arm insignia. His British leather jerkin and M1918 hobnailed boots are of note.

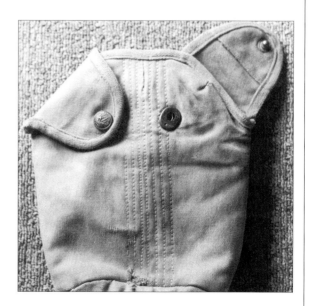

ABOVE **Canteen cover with snap fasteners bearing the USMC EGA device. Though illegible in the photo, manufacturer information is evident on the inside of the flap. (MCRD)**

LEFT **Gny.Sgt. Wiman and Capt.Lytle of the 1st Marine Aviation Force in October 1918; Wiman wears the French flying suit with a fur collar, Lytle a leather coat (see also Plate H). Half this unit's pilots were Navy Reserve flyers commissioned into the Marines.**

Plate G: Argonne, November 1918:

G1 Grenadier, 4th Brigade The unlined raincoat was supplied to the AEF to replace the poncho for foul weather use. It was well liked, and was sometimes used in the summer as a dustcoat. Here, a Marine wears it for warmth as well as protection from the damp. His Springfield 03 is fitted with the modified French VB grenade launching cup. He would probably carry the grenades in a haversack, although an 11-pocket tie-on apron was also issued and usually worn on one hip. This private also has a US-designed, French-made brass knuckle fighting knife (Mk I) fitted to his belt. His gasmask bag has been decorated with the 2nd Division's star and Indianhead insignia, soon to be seen as a shoulder patch.

G2 Assistant Browning Gunner, 5th Marines
This private wears the P1917 Marine uniform, which at this date shows him to be a recently arrived replacement. He is dressed lightly for this November battle, and must hope for quick access to an overcoat or blanket once he stops moving and his unit consolidates. He wears an assistant gunner's cartridge belt which has pouches for both rifle clips and 20-round magazines for the Browning automatic rifle; he also carries a bandoleer of 50 additional 30-06 rounds across his chest (both the 03 and the 'light Browning' used 30-06). His job is to stay by the gunner, providing him with ammunition as needed, and to take over the weapon should the gunner go down.

G3 Browning Gunner, 5th Marines
This veteran private first class displays two overseas stripes and one wound stripe on the tunic cuffs of his standard AEF drab uniform. He is lucky in having been issued with one of the new light Browning automatic rifles; the Marine Brigade did not receive a full scale of these excellent weapons – the best of their class to come out of the war – until after the Armistice. The gunner's belt illustrated carried eight Browning and two pistol magazines, and this gunner carries his .45 in the M1916 russet holster. The sling and the belt with a metal butt cup were specially designed to allow firing from the hip while moving.

Plate H: Insignia:

H1 Marine collar disks similar to the Army pattern were manufactured by French and US sources. They began to become available at the time of the Armistice. German-made disks were also produced in 1919.

H2 Helmet with 2nd Division HQ marking and EGA, as worn on victory parades in New York and Washington DC.

H3 Black- and purple-backed 2nd Div patches, as worn by 4th Bde HQ and 6th MG Bn.

H4 2nd Div patches as worn by 5th Marine Regt, respectively: HQ, 1st, 2nd, 3rd Bns, MG Co, Supply Co.

H5 2nd Div patches as worn by 6th Marine Regt, respectively: HQ, 1st, 2nd, 3rd Bns, MG Co, Supply Co.

H6 US Navy Aviator wings as worn by Marine flyers.

H7 5th Bde patch and vehicle insignia (first pattern), c.1919.

H8 5th Bde, 11th Marine Regt patch (second pattern), c.1919.

H9 Victory Medal ribbon with five battle stars; Victory Medal with five battle clasps: Aisne, Aisne-Marne, St Mihiel, Meuse-Argonne and Defensive Sector.

H10 Captain, 1st Marine Aviation Force, 1918 This aviator wears a US-issue leather flying coat; also commonly worn was a French one-piece lined canvas flying suit. His overseas cap shows Marine red piping as worn by officers. He has put the smaller collar rank badge on his cap and has left off the EGA. The DH-4 or DH-9A fuselage detail shows the national roundel insignia with the addition of the EGA device. A shoulder patch with this insignia was planned, but it is doubtful that it was ever produced.